Drawing Cartoons Letter by Letter

Drawing Cartoons Letter by Letter

Create Fun Characters from A to Z

Mixed Media Resources
New York

Christopher Hart Books for KIDS

An imprint of
Mixed Media Resources
161 Avenue of the Americas
New York, NY 10013

Editorial Director
JOAN KRELLENSTEIN

Senior Editor
MICHELLE BREDESON

Managing Editor
LAURA COOKE

Art Director
IRENE LEDWITH

Book Design
JULIE GRANT

Editorial Assistant
JACOB SEIFERT

Production
J. ARTHUR MEDIA

Vice President
TRISHA MALCOLM

Publisher
CARRIE KILMER

Production Manager
DAVID JOINNIDES

President
ART JOINNIDES

Chairman
JAY STEIN

FOR everyone who loves to draw.

Library of Congress Cataloging-in-Publication Data
Names: Hart, Christopher, 1957- author.
Title: Drawing cartoons letter by letter : create fun characters from A to Z / by Christopher Hart.
Description: First edition. | New York, NY : Drawing with Christopher Hart, 2017. | Includes index.
Identifiers: LCCN 2016039234 | ISBN 9781942021537 (pbk.)
Subjects: LCSH: Cartoon characters in art. | Lettering in art. | Cartooning--Technique.
Classification: LCC NC1764 .H359 2017 | DDC 741.5/1--dc23
LC record available at https://lccn.loc.gov/2016039234
Printed in China.
1 3 5 7 9 10 8 6 4 2

•••

christopherhartbooks.com

What's Inside

Drawing Is as Easy as ABC!

Welcome, artists!

In my best-selling books *Drawing Shape by Shape* and *Drawing Shape by Shape: Animals* I showed you how to take simple circles, squares, and triangles and turn them into hundreds of cute animals, funny people, and cartoony things. In this book, I'll do the same thing with the letters of the alphabet. You'll see them transform in front of your eyes into cartoon characters such as kings, fashion models, nerdy dads, and more. It's like creating magic with a pencil. And you're the magician!

I'll show you how you can take a D, or a K, or any letter, and draw all kinds of characters. I've included enough simple steps so you can get the same amazing results you see here.

All you need to begin is a pencil. We'll start each character with a letter then add a few lines at each step. Once your drawing is the way you like it, you can add color, like I did, to make the cartoon stand out. You'll soon be creating dozens of original cartoon characters. Let's get started!

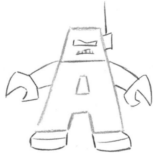

Happy Drawing!
Christopher Hart

Cute witch

Robot from Galaxy X

Defender of justice

Got it on sale

Chic chapeau

Cool guy

The first snowfall

B is for bee

Cheery grandma

Advisor to the queen

Funny dragon

"Oh no!!"

En pointe

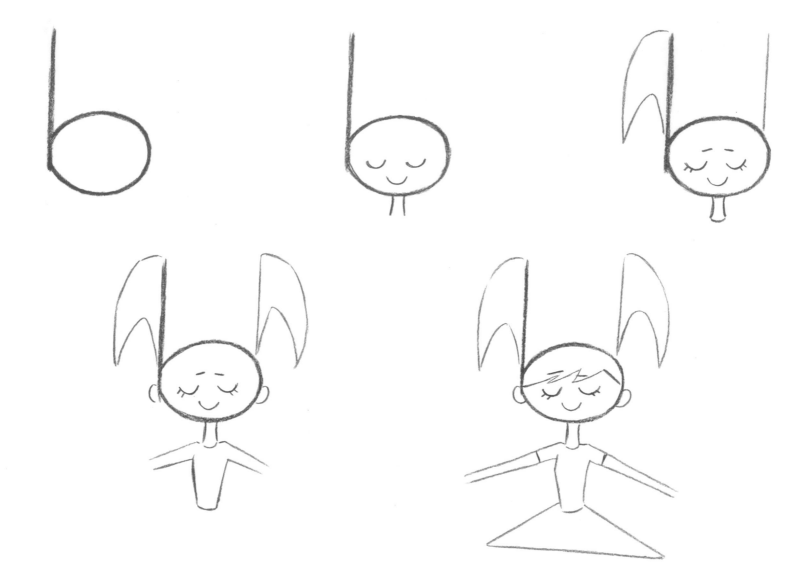

up to no good

Shy girl

Happy dad

"Can you keep a secret?"

Psst—

Dinosaur dash

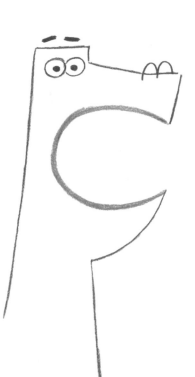

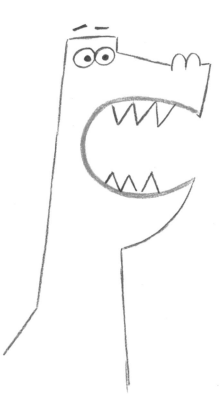

Nervous knight

Glamour girl

Little ladybug

"Kale for dinner?!"

Grumpy Gary

"I forgot my password!"

Soldier

Stylish lady

"Can I have a hug?"

Guilty look

Cityscape

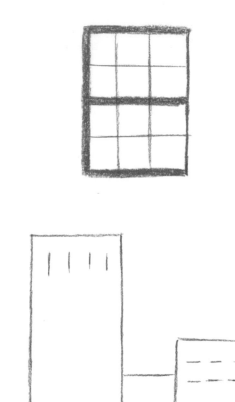

Buttoned up

Little Leaguer

Scrubbed and ready

"Did I remember to lock the castle door?"

Stubborn Sam

Pretty pleased

Little lady, big personality

Perfect posture

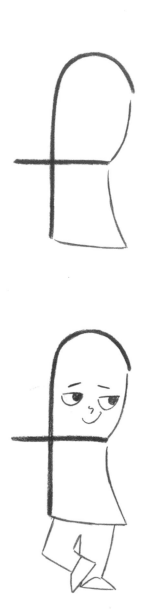

Knowing smile

Summer hat

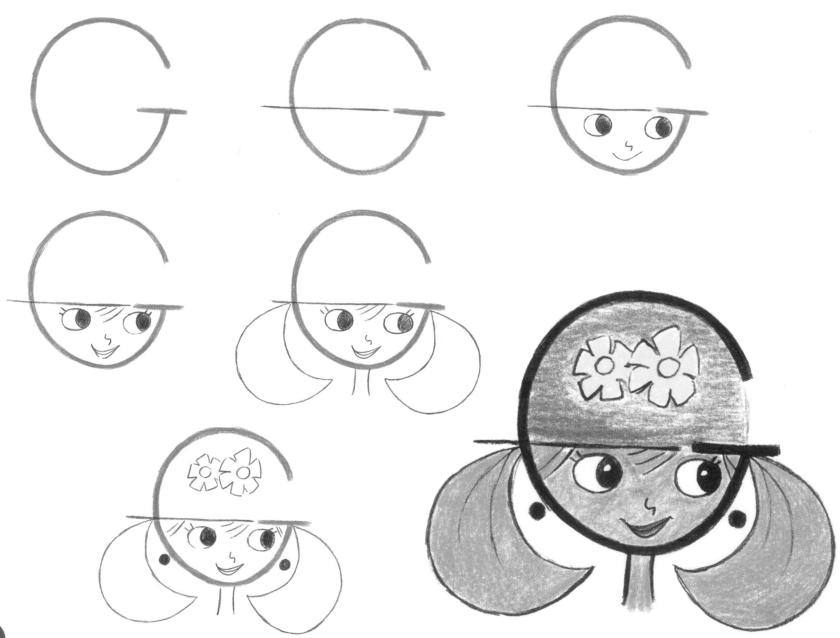

Coffee break

"For you, madame?"

In hot water

Super ponytail

Coach dad

Cool and casual

Know-it-all

Spike

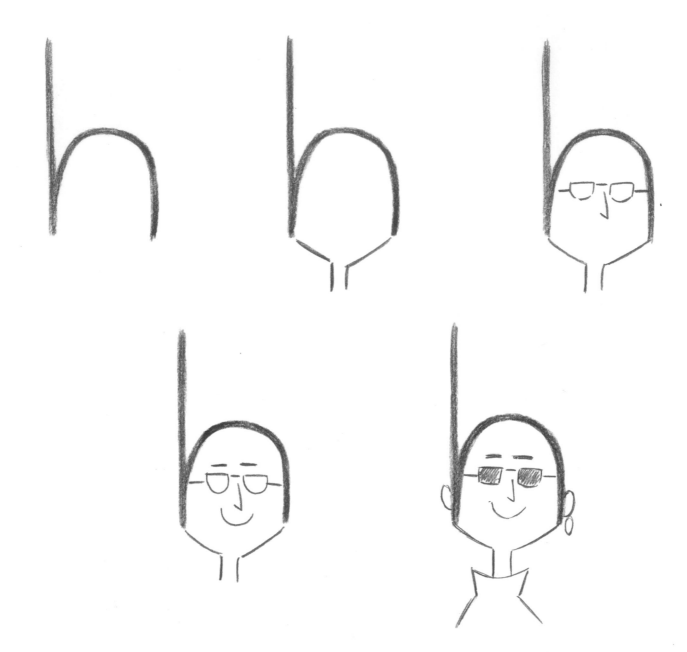

Friendly girl

Girl with headband

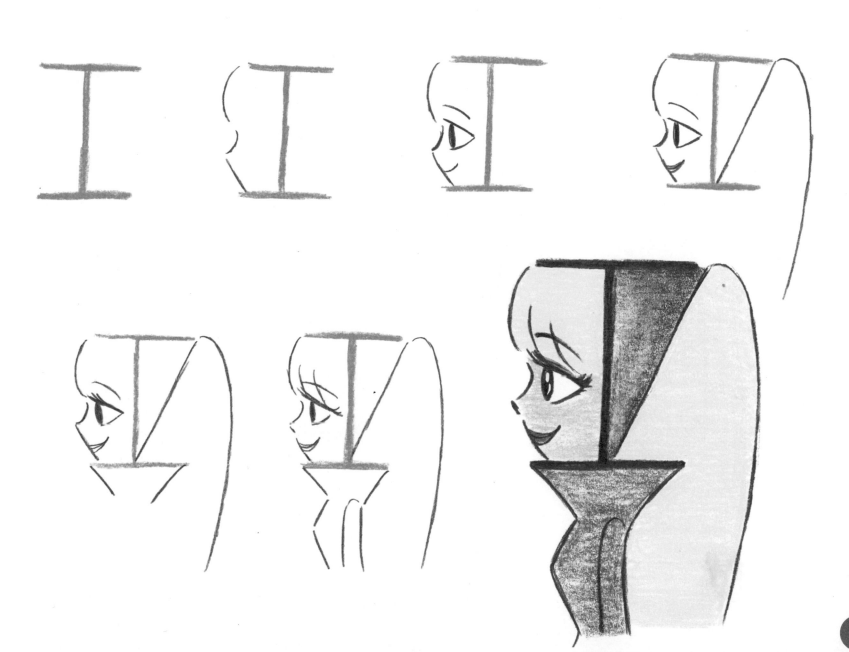

Amazing brainy head

The general

So trendy!

Taking the human for a walk

Surprised

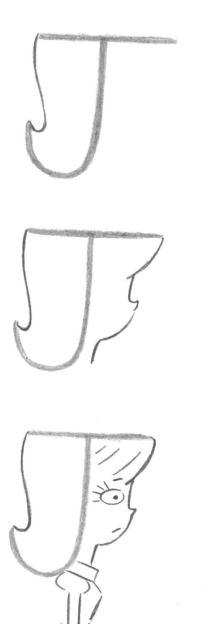

Sporty guy

Secret service agent

Southwest landscape

Ready for bed!

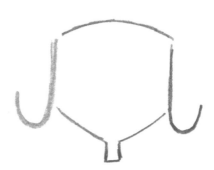

Not as cool as he thinks he is

Spooky and kooky

Runway ready

Fun lesson

rhomboid

zzz

Island warrior

"you forgot someone!!"

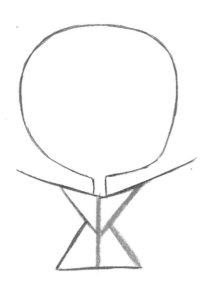

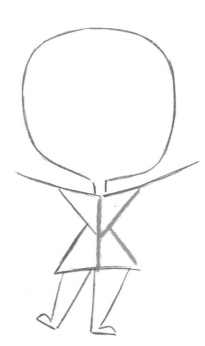

Blockhead

Shy smile

93

Simple hand

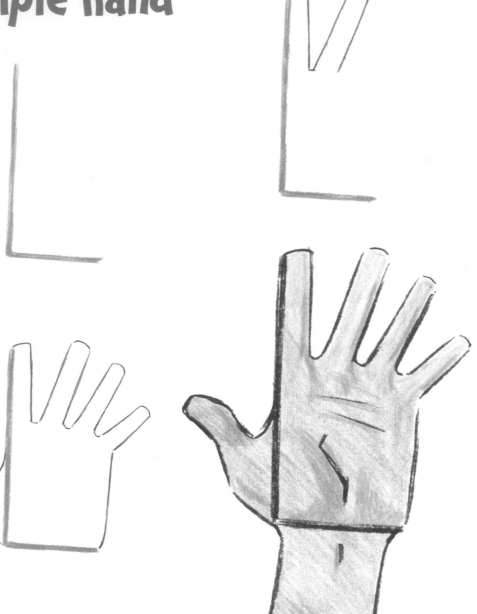

Zoom!

Goofy guy

"Eeeeek!"

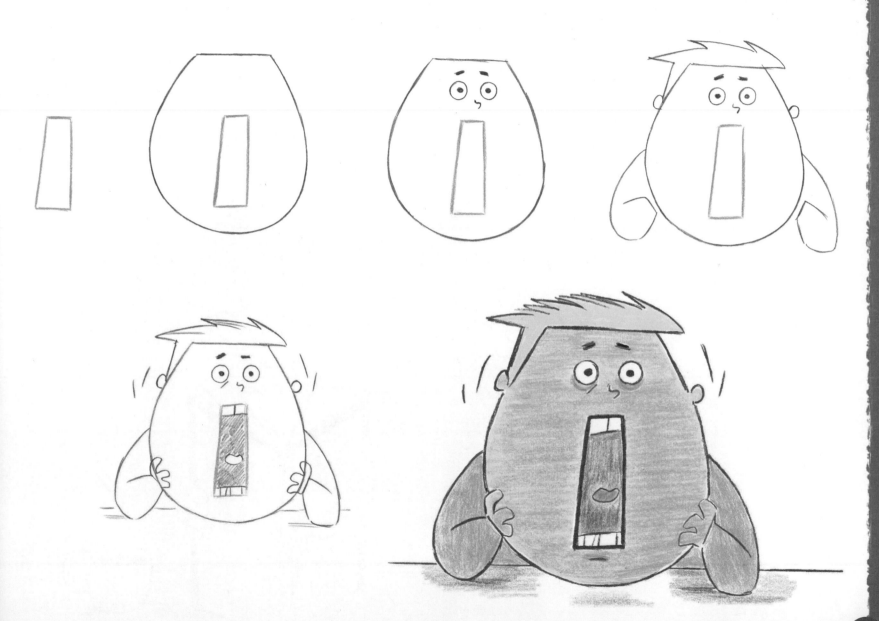

"Where's my sports section?!"

Open mic night

Super spy

"Someday I'll be a cartoonist..."

"The paper is due tomorrow?!?"

"Happy Halloween!"

The latest hairstyle

Morning pick-me-up

Honor student

Under the sea

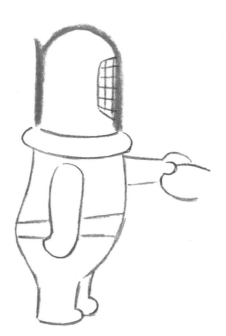

Feeling antsy

Winter glamour

Mystery man

Undercover agent

Cute and little

Aspiring director

"But I was promised the corner office!"

Got trees?

P

ultra chic

Mad scientist

Can burp the alphabet

Pretty in pink

The graduate

"See ya later!"

Secret mission

Soccer star

"Let's see... Where did I park?"

Colorful lady

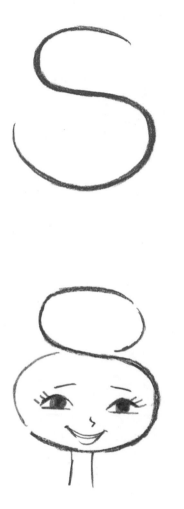

Funny kid

"Cheer up, little guy!"

Big chin

S

Opera singer

Wide-eyed girl

Morning mom

Sunglasses

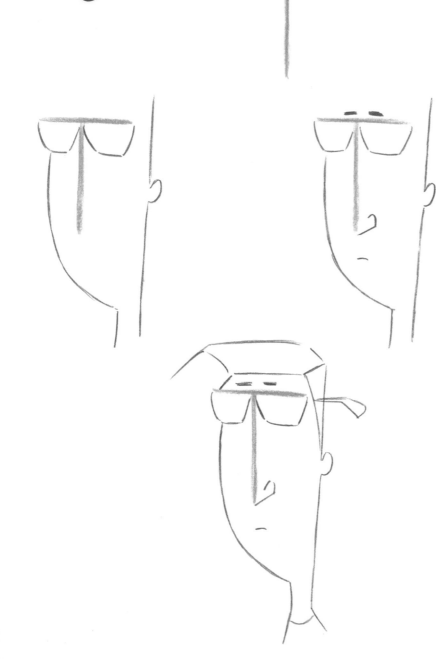

Bright idea

Pretty lady

"Marry me!"

Computer geek

Cosplay kid

The smallest princess

Future candy dish

WINNER

Surf's up!

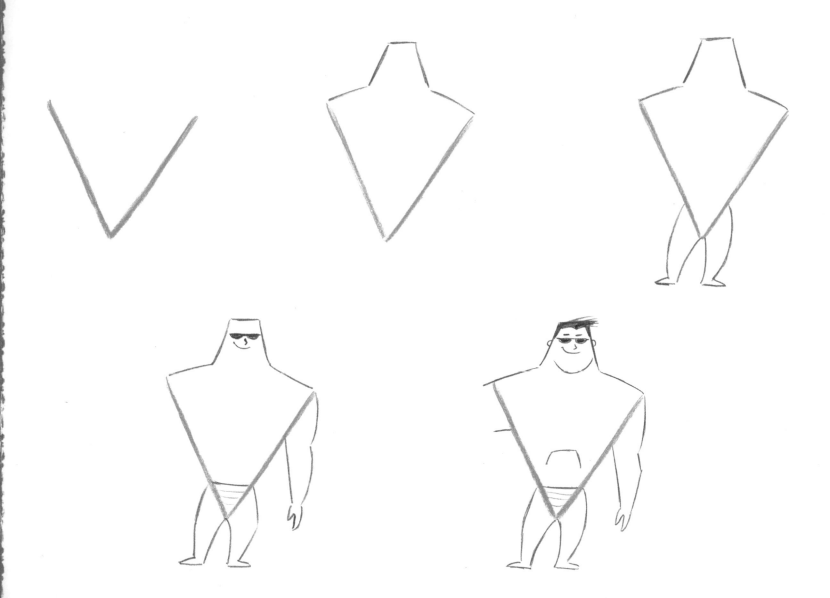

Trying to look stylish (keep trying!)

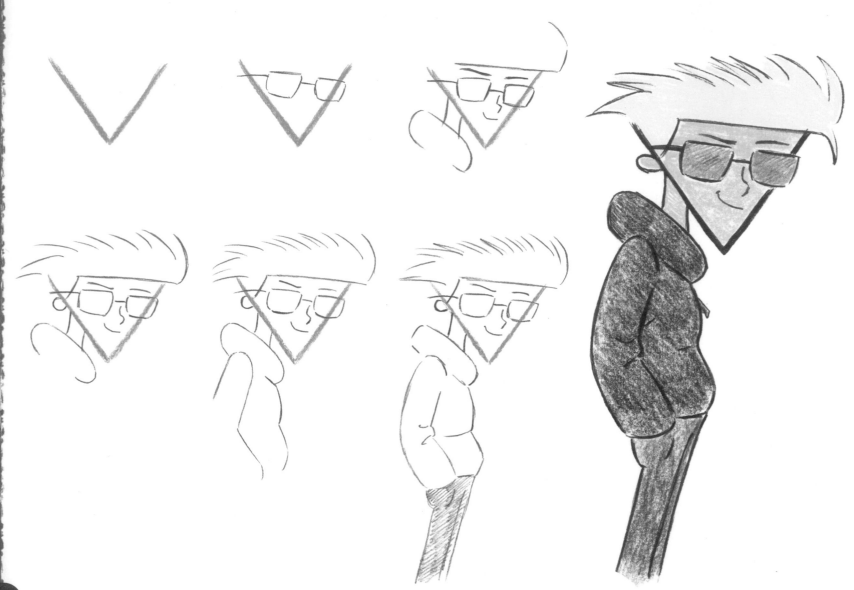

Big smile

Good-natured dad

Hipster

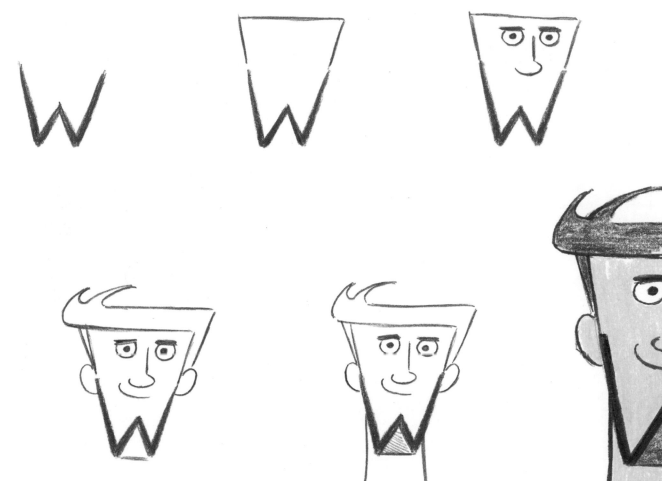

On the catwalk

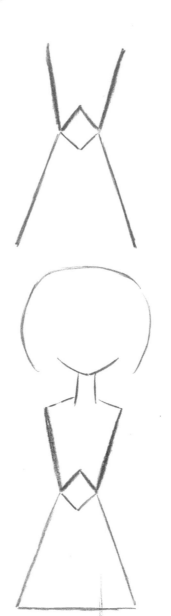

"Hello, darling!"

Goofy grin

Proton power

City stroll

Teacher's pet

Lovey dovey

Kiss ♥

College student

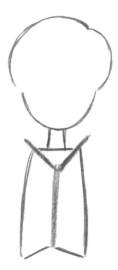

Sorceress

One happy guy

Friendly guy

"Anyone seen my horse?"

Sharp haircut

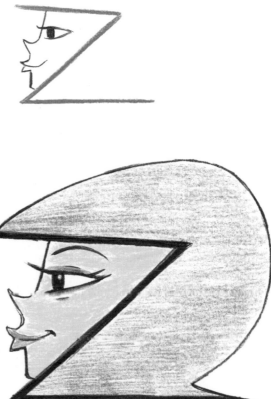

Bad mood dude

"Pleased to meet ya!"

Looking for your favorite character?

Check the alphabetical list to see which page it's on.

Index

Learn to Draw with Simple Shapes!

Chris Hart Books for KIDS

Drawing Shape by Shape
Create Cartoon Characters with Circles, Squares & Triangles

Christopher Hart Books for KIDS

DRAWING ANIMALS Shape by Shape
Create Cartoon Animals with Circles, Squares, Rectangles & Triangles

Connect with Chris on Facebook at facebook.com/learn.to.draw.cartoons.
Available wherever books are sold or at sixthandspringbooks.com.